How to Grow Dahlias

JOHN ALLPORT

Copyright © 2014 John Allport

All rights reserved.

ISBN-13: 978-1499118667

CONTENTS

1. Preparing the Ground — Pg. 1

   Drainage, Soil Type, Location, Soil Condition

2. Planting — Pg. 7

   Time of Planting, Soil Conditions, Marking Out and Staking Beds, Selection of Tubers, Labels, Planting

3. Early Season Care — Pg. 15

   Time of Emergence, Protection of Shoots, Watering, Tying, Tuber Rot, Feeding

4. General Cultivation — Pg. 21

   Obtaining Plants, Colours, Form, Pruning and Disbudding, Pests and Diseases

5. Feeding and Watering — Pg. 29

   Feeding, Chemical Fertilizers, Organic Fertilizers, Liquid Fertilizers, A Feeding Program, Watering

6. Propagation — Pg. 45

   Growing from Seeds, Growing from Tubers, Growing from Cuttings, Method of Producing Green Plants

7. Lifting, Dividing and Storing Tubers — Pg. 51

   Need to Lift Tubers, Time of Lifting, Lifting Procedures, Dividing Tuber Clumps, Storage of Divided Tubers, Storage of Tuber Clumps, Common Problems, Garden Hygiene

1 PREPARING THE GROUND

The ideal situation for growing dahlias is in separate well-drained beds of deep, rich loamy soil in an open sunny position which is sheltered from winds and frosts. This, of course, is the type of location which suits the majority of flowering plants. Unfortunately it is rare to find any garden where these conditions prevail throughout the entire area. The dahlias will therefore have to accept some compromise and share the ideal conditions with the other plants in the garden, but perhaps with some effort to improve any circumstances which are unsatisfactory. To make such improvements the relative importance of the various needs of the dahlia should be considered.

Dahlias grow better in beds of their own rather than being mixed with other plant species and the cultivation methods of dahlias, such as lifting annually, will often preclude the sharing of beds. If only a small number of plants are to be grown it is preferable to find a small bed in a sunny corner rather than dotting dahlias among other plants. Where larger numbers are involved the use of separate beds is the most satisfactory method, and if being grown for show purposes separate beds are definitely required.

DRAINAGE

Good drainage is the most important requirement and some attention should be paid to this. There are many ways of improving drainage - agricultural pipes, flexible drainage hose and trenches, but the easiest way is by raising the beds. The use of 200 to 250 mm boards on edge with the soil being built up to this level above the surrounding ground is a common method, but even the heaping of soil as the bed is being dug is a help providing a trench is left at the edge of the bed and water can escape.

SOIL TYPE

Dahlias will grow in almost any type of soil, but it must be friable enough for the roots and tubers to develop and rich enough to provide the substantial amount of nutrition that the dahlia likes. This is best achieved by placing liberal quantities of manures, compost, straw, decaying leaves, grass clippings and any other organic material on the beds during winter and digging this in during early spring.

Another way of improving both the texture and nutrient content of the soil is by the use of a green crop. This is a crop of selected species sown as soon as the beds can be cleared, grown during the winter and dug into the ground at least four weeks before the final preparation of beds. For dahlias oats and rye-corn are suitable, but as these utilise nitrogen in both growing and rotting down it would be wise to include a legume such as tick beans or field peas to grow at the same time.

Any manures placed on the beds during winter can be fresh, but manure used in the spring should be well matured. The use of fresh manure at any time is frowned on by some leading growers, especially poultry manure which should be at least twelve months old before it is used.

LOCATION

Dahlias are sun lovers and will thrive in full sun but will grow successfully with as little as six or seven hours a day, especially if they receive morning sun. They certainly will not thrive in full shade, and if grown close to high fences or under shrubs or trees they will be drawn and tall with long weak stems. If some plants must be grown in areas where they receive less than full sun it would be prudent to choose for those locations varieties which need shading for best results. It will be found that red and orange blooms are apt to fade in strong sun but, curiously, the colour of most pink blooms is strengthened by the sun.

The growth of dahlias is of a hollow-stemmed nature and is very brittle. This, together with the immense weight of flowers and foliage at the height of their growing period, makes them very vulnerable to strong winds which can devastate plants. If a sheltered position is not available then this must be recognised and extra attention paid to staking and tying.

Protection from frost, if such a thing is possible, is a bonus. Most districts have a regular climate pattern and planting times are arranged accordingly. Beginners should find out the normal planting times from experienced growers and grow their plants at the same time.

SOIL CONDITION

If new beds are being made the more effort put into the task the better will be the results. Although the soil may be basically good it will still need some work to create a suitable texture and ensure a sufficient supply of nutrients. It would be expected that new ground that has not been cultivated for some years will be dug over three times before planting is done, each digging producing a finer texture than the previous one.

Where established beds are concerned the building up of the soil should continue to ensure a constant supply of nutrients. Dahlias are gross feeders and it is difficult to overfeed them with the use of matured organic fertilizer provided that this is not too fresh. Dahlias can occupy the same ground for many years. It is known that some beds have been used year after year for over forty years and have continued to produce the highest quality blooms. The secret of this is that each year they have had three or four inches of stable manure added to them.

When adding any materials to the soil there is always a likelihood of changing not only the structure and nutrient value but also the acidity. The acidity of soil is measured by a scale known as the Ph scale on which neutral is a reading of 7. Any number below this indicates an acid condition and a number greater than 7 shows that the soil is alkaline. Dahlias will grow well in soils in the range 6 to 7.5, with 6.75 being the preferred level. For new beds it is advisable to obtain a Ph reading to find out whether any corrective action is required and to seek advice on how to achieve this. It is a simple matter to reduce soil acidity by the application of lime and to increase acidity with sulphur, but the exact quantities to use require a special study. It is usual to give beds a dressing of dolomite lime every winter at the rate of about one handful to each square meter to compensate for the use of normal quantities of manure and maintain the Ph level. Apart from this any attempt to change Ph levels should only be made after seeking specialised advice.

Many of the organic materials which would be of use in improving the texture of the soil also have other effects. Pine bark, sawdust and pine needles, for example, will not only increase soil acidity but will also use vast amounts of nitrogen while they are decomposing. This will create a nitrogen deficiency, which is a problem in itself, and many of the means of introducing extra nitrogen will raise the acidity level. It will be seen therefore that a great deal of care should be exercised when changing the nature of the soil.

The beginner should not be put off by this. The majority of soils are quite suitable for the growing of dahlias, with their comparatively wide range of tolerance, provided that there is no attempt to make drastic changes. Large quantities of compost and well-rotted manure will not do a great deal of harm if accompanied by a light application of lime, but a similar quantity of sawdust could do a lot of harm. If there are any doubts or worries about this aspect of the soil it would be wise to invest in a Ph testing kit.

The soil in beds should be cultivated to a moderately fine texture. It is not necessary to get it to seed-bed fineness, but soil which is made up of large lumps of clay will not yield good results. Although dahlias have a fairly large root system, and produce a substantial clump of tubers, they are not particularly deep rooted. If the soil is cultivated to a good spade depth and the sub-soil is fairly loose this should suffice.

2 PLANTING

TIME OF PLANTING

The time for planting dahlias is in the spring, the precise part of the spring being dependant on your location. In cold or cool climates the temperatures could well be quite cold in early spring and no purpose would be served in planting at this time. Many losses occur when tubers sit in cold wet ground waiting for the warm weather to get them started. In this situation mid-spring would be a more suitable time. In warm and hot areas very early spring would be more suitable, and it will be found that under these conditions the plants will grow more quickly, mature faster, and come to the end of their season earlier. Other dahlia growers in the area will be able to give guidance on this, but remember that even local variations in climate can be considerable. There is probably more danger in planting early than planting late providing the planting is completed by the end of spring. Those who are growing for show purposes will need to be a little more accurate than this but will also have some experience on which to base their planting times. The beginner would be wise to take note of planting dates and the blooming times from these plantings for future reference. Should it be necessary to make late plantings because of losses or obtaining new tubers late then plantings can be made up to mid-summer. The flowering season for these plants will be very short, but the tubers produced could be useful.

Even the most experienced growers frequently have their plans upset by unusual weather conditions in certain years, and it is common in dahlia circles to see many worried looks in early summer because it has been too dry, too wet, too hot or too cold. Eventually everything turns out well and gardens, vases and show benches are filled with dahlias at the appropriate times.

SOIL CONDITIONS

Prior to planting the soil should have been well-worked into a moderately fine tilth, free from any weed growth and debris left over from the previous year. Some growers like to incorporate some of the fertilizer they intend to use at this stage, either over the entire bed or at the points where the plants are to grow. If the fertilizer is to be applied to the whole of the bed it should be broadcast on the surface and lightly raked in. At the time of planting the soil should be fairly moist, and in spring there is not often a problem with the soil being too dry. If a dry spell should be experienced the beds may be watered, but in doing this bear in mind that rain could follow and the result would be very wet beds. Any watering should therefore be minimal. Should the soil be very wet it would be best to delay planting for a little while until it dries out.

MARKING OUT AND STAKING BEDS

When the bed is ready for planting the stakes should be driven into the ground at the required distance apart. This distance should be between 700 mm and 900 mm, anything less than this is starting to overcrowd the plants and anything greater is unnecessarily generous. Where beds are 1.2 meters or more in width two rows of plants may be grown, the plants being staggered in the rows. Even wider beds could take three rows, but unless the bed can be reached from both sides anything greater than this will make it difficult to tend the plants without causing damage.

It is important to drive in the stakes before the tubers are planted. It is only too easy to impale a tuber if they are placed when the tubers are already in the ground. The stakes should be at least 30 mm square and driven at least 350 mm into the ground, and should be between 900 mm and 1200 mm above ground. Remember that this stake will be called upon to support a plant which can be almost two meters high. Many gardeners soak their stakes in oil, creosote, or similar substances to prolong their life. While this is sound practice, any surplus preservative should be removed before the stake is used. Should any of this substance be washed into the ground the effect on the tender young roots would be disastrous.

If it has been decided to incorporate some of the fertilizers to be used into the soil under the plants then this is the time to do it. A hole should be made in front of the stake where the plant will be, about a spade's depth is deep enough. The fertilizer should be sprinkled into this hole and thoroughly worked into the soil before the hole is back-filled. Care should be taken that fresh fertilizer will not come into contact with the tender new roots as they grow from the tuber or the roots of a green plant.

SELECTION OF TUBERS

Tubers which are very large are not necessarily the best to plant, and those people who go to tuber sales and feel that they have done well because they have purchased enormous tubers have done themselves no favours. The tuber is the food store which will nourish the plant until it has made sufficient roots to support itself, and it follows therefore that a plant which is drawing on this food store for a long period will be likely to delay the formation of roots until that store has become depleted. The formation of roots early in the growing period will ensure a better root system to support the plant until the end of its life, and will also provide a better crop of tubers for the following year. The ideal size for a tuber would be between 75 mm to 150 mm although some varieties produce quite small tubers of only 50 mm which are perfectly suitable. Some growers will reduce the size of tubers which are greater than about 200 mm by cutting off the excess. If this is done the cut end must be treated with sulphur. More important than size is the condition of the tuber which should be plump, smooth skinned, and free from any signs of rotting, with at least one healthy looking eye or bud.

LABELS

It is at planting time that the labelling of plants is first done, and the work at this stage will determine whether all the varieties will retain their identification or will become just another collection of unnamed dahlias which cannot be exchanged, sold, given away, shown in competition or replanted with any confidence. To a serious dahlia grower an unnamed plant or tuber is almost worthless, for to establish its identity will require it to be grown for an entire year after which it may be found to be a duplication of a variety of which ample plantings have already been made.

The method of labelling can help in some of the operations which will be carried out during the season. Permanent labels made of metal with the name painted on and fixed to the stake with wire will not only serve for many seasons but will also be convenient for fixing to tuber clumps at lifting time. Labels which are coded by colour, or some other means, which identifies the type and size of the variety will assist the beginner (who probably cannot remember all the new varieties by size and type) when it is time to disbud the plants to get show standard blooms.

Whatever method is used the label should be durable and the marker used to inscribe the name should be not only waterproof but fade proof, and in this respect it is better to take the advice of an experienced grower rather than that of the seller of the marker. The practice of writing the name of the variety on the stake can (and has) caused a great deal of confusion, and to retain stakes for the same varieties year after year is not the simple proposition it at first seems.

All labels should be prepared before planting begins, and is a job which can be carried out during the winter to save valuable time in the spring. No experienced grower would think of planting a plant or tuber without the proper label being at hand, for the human memory is too fallible for any reliance to be placed upon it. The first action when starting to plant tubers should be to place the tuber or plant next to the stake and fix the correct label to the stake. In this way all plants will be correctly labelled.

PLANTING

Where green plants (plants grown from cuttings), or tubers gown in pots, are concerned there is very little difference between planting the dahlia and any other plant, except to remember that the dahlia is frost-tender. Planting depth will be to the natural level at which the plant was growing in its pot, the stem of the young plant will be about 30 to 40 mm from the stake, the soil will be firmed around the plant to make a slight depression, and the plant will be watered. Planting is best carried out during late afternoon or evening, and if the sun is likely to be strong a little shade should be provided for a couple of days. If the plant is well grown (150 mm or more) the first tie should be made, this being a loose tie which gives support without pulling the plant towards the stake.

If tubers are being planted a supply of sharp, salt-free sand should be available, and a hole scooped out from in front of the stake and lined with about 25 mm of this sand. The hole should be such that the tuber will lie in it almost horizontally with the eye end a little higher than the rest of the tuber, the eye being about 30 to 40 mm from the stake.

The depth of planting is a subject that seems to worry many new growers, and there have been quite a number of opinions given on this question. Having seen perfectly good plants growing from tubers that have been accidentally buried and from tubers that have been left on top of the ground it may well be that the planting depth is not as critical as we have been led to believe. As a general rule hot climates indicate a need for deeper planting, as do light soils, whereas cooler climates and heavier soils call for less depth. In sandy soil in a hot climate the planting depth would be 160 mm and in a cool climate plantings in heavy soil would be in the region of 75 mm. Having placed the tuber on its sandy bed with the eye pointing up at the appropriate depth a further layer of sand should be placed on top of the tuber, at the eye end. This layer should be thick enough to come up to soil level. The benefits of this sand are that it protects the tuber from attack by wireworms, improves the drainage, provides an easy passage for the emerging shoot, creates a good root run for the roots as they develop and ensures that the tubers are clean when lifting time comes. In addition the incorporation of sand year after year will improve the texture of heavy soils.

After planting is completed some form of slug and snail killer should be placed on the beds. These pests can do a lot of damage to the emerging shoots, even going a little way below ground to meet them, and by starting to eradicate them early the losses from this source will be reduced. There have been many tubers which have been considered as having failed to shoot when the shoots have in fact been eaten by slugs or snails. When using slug and snail killers, particularly in pellet form, the utmost care should be taken to ensure that it is not eaten by children or animals. There are a number of ways to use this substance safely, but one of the better ways is to lay the bait in short lengths of 50 mm tubing. There are other methods of ridding the garden of these pests, ranging from various recipes such as stale beer to allowing poultry to roam the area. Whatever means is used is not as important as the fact that they must be controlled. A dahlia patch with snails will not produce good dahlias but will produce a very frustrated grower.

3 EARLY SEASON CARE

The care which is given to the young dahlia plants in the first couple of months is crucial, not only to the quality of the plants which will bear the crop of spectacular flowers but in determining whether there will be a crop at all. The new grower, in particular, will be anxious to see signs of growth, full of questions on whether the plants are progressing well and seeking to do something that will help things along a little. There are questions that can be answered and procedures to ensure that plants get a good start in life, and there are problems that can arise that must be attended to. Even the most hardened veteran of the dahlia world gets a lot of satisfaction from seeing another year's crop rising from the ground to form healthy bushes. Many, but not all, of the early problems relate to tuber plantings, where the important activity is happening underground, and it is in this area that some advice can be given.

TIME OF EMERGENCE

The question of how long shoots from tubers take to emerge is a vexed one. Briefly, a lot depends on the time of planting, the weather conditions, the depth of planting, the state of advancement of the tuber at planting time and the variety. In general the shoots should be expected to come through about four weeks after planting and up until this time patience should be exercised. There is always a temptation to poke around the tuber to see if a shoot is growing but this is perhaps one of the best ways to make sure it does not grow, for there have been many good tubers ruined by having the shoots knocked off by careless fingers. If, after four weeks, there is no sign of growth then an investigation can be made, an operation that should be carried out very gently. One way of doing this is to feel for the end of the tuber opposite the eye and work the fingers under the tuber until the eye end is reached. The sand can then be removed to reveal whether there is a shoot. Perhaps a safer way is to take a spade and carefully lift the entire area around the tuber. If this is done slowly the sand will fall away from the tuber and reveal the eye or shoot. As soon as a shoot is sighted the tuber should be lowered gently back into place and covered with sand. If there is no sign of a shoot then the tuber must be lifted out. If the eye is still sound the tuber should be replanted but if the eye is showing no sign of life or the tuber has rotted it must be replaced. It is not at all unusual for some apparently good tubers to fail and for this reason it is always wise to keep a few tubers or plants in reserve for use as replacements.

PROTECTION OF SHOOTS

As shoots come through they are robust enough to continue growing without any assistance provided they are not subjected to any interference. The problem of slugs and snails has already been discussed and it is essential that the protection continues. There are other threats to the small shoots, birds love to use the sand as a bath, cats find other uses for it, dogs may trespass on the beds, and in some areas other small animals may wander around the garden. Although these creatures may have no malicious intent they are quite likely to damage the young shoots and with them any chance of future growth. There are some growers who place small sticks around the young shoots to protect them, and others who use broken plant pots without bottoms or small cardboard cartons without tops or bottoms to place over the shoots. Where milk is sold in cartons these make ideal shields and also tend to keep the slugs and snails at bay.

WATERING

It was previously explained that the tuber gives enough nourishment to last the tuber until it forms roots and the same thing applies to moisture. Tubers should not be watered until the shoots or young plants are about 75 to 100 mm high, by which time they will have started to grow roots. To apply water before this stage will do nothing to encourage growth and could lead to the rotting of the tubers. The only time when watering should be considered is during a very dry spell when the ground is quite dry to a depth of 100 mm.

The comments regarding watering do not apply to green plants which need to be kept moist at all times. Where a mixture of tubers and green plants are in the same bed the green plants will need to be watered individually

TYING

The first tie should be made when the plant is about 200 mm to 250 mm high. Although there is little weight to support, the tying of plants at this stage will help to prevent them from being blown around and becoming loose in the ground. The security given to the plants appears to improve the rate of growth. Shortly after placing the tie it will be noticed that the young plant takes on a new lease of life and increases in height and in the thickness of the stem. The tie which is made at this early stage should not be tight nor should it attempt to draw the stem of the plant to the stake. The twine used should be fairly thick. Binder twine is quite satisfactory and has an inherent stiffness which gives support. When making this first tie it is helpful to use a bow or knot that can be released easily because this tie must be removed as the stem starts to swell.

TUBER ROT

One of the most disappointing events in the growing of dahlias is when tuber rot strikes young plants. The problem arises because the tuber starts to rot after growth has started and the toxic nature of the decaying tuber poisons the plant which will eventually die. The problem can appear at any time from when the shoot is only 50 mm high until it is a plant of 300 mm high. The symptoms of this are that the plant ceases to grow or grows extremely slowly and the foliage takes on a dark blue-green colour with a lack-lustre appearance. This condition can often be cured, especially if it is tackled as soon as the symptoms are recognised, although the treatment may seem rather drastic.

The first thing to do is to confirm the diagnosis by feeling for the end of the tuber below ground and establishing if rot is present. This will be evidenced by a soft mushy feel to the tuber, and if this is found to be the case the tuber and small plant must be lifted. If the plant is large a slightly different method must be used.

When the plant is out of the ground all trace of the rotten tuber must be cut away. If the rot is extensive all of the tuber must be removed and the shoot used to strike as a cutting, but if a root system has developed the tuber can be removed and what amounts to a green plant will be left for planting.

Where a larger plant of 200 mm or over is concerned it would not survive being removed from the ground. In such a case the soil must be gently scraped from around the tuber and any rotten tuber cut away with as little disturbance as possible. Most plants of this size will have a fairly well developed root system and with a good watering should survive.

Tuber rot will not affect plants which originated as green plants, which is another advantage in using this method of increasing stock.

FEEDING

If the ground has been well-prepared there should be no need to provide any further nutrients until the plants have grown to about 300 mm high, and only then if the planned program of feeding is based on side dressings of fertilizer. In most situations the growth will be regulated by the temperature and any feeding would do more harm than good. The temptation to boost growth with liquid fertilizer with a high nitrogen content should be resisted. When the days grow longer, the sun is a little stronger, and the plants have grown to the stage where the roots are becoming established, the plants will grow at a most satisfactory rate.

4 GENERAL CULTIVATION

The gardener who wishes to grow dahlias as a means of producing colour in the garden and has little or no interest in growing blooms to show standard might regard some of the information in this book as unnecessary, and up to a point this notion is valid. However, a great deal of the subject matter in other chapters applies to the growing of dahlias for all purposes, and it would be advisable to look at the information given and use it for your own needs.

This chapter is intended as a basic introduction for those who wish to get on with the task of filling their gardens with colourful flowers before becoming involved in the more technical aspects of dahlia growing. Some of the techniques of growing will vary but in general the basic culture will not change a great deal. The main considerations will be colour, size, type and quantity of blooms, rather than conformation with the standards laid down for show blooms. It should be remembered that even though the primary use may be to create a spectacular effect in the garden there will be times when some blooms will be required for cutting and some varieties suitable for this purpose should be considered.

The dahlia is an ideal plant to use for garden display. The range of sizes, forms and colours are unsurpassed and the plants will bloom from early summer until the end of autumn in many areas. The gardener who is using dahlias for this purpose will not be seeking the same characteristics as the exhibitor, as quantity will take precedence over quality. Nevertheless, there is no need for inferior varieties to be chosen. The flowers that the exhibitor stages on the show bench so proudly will usually also produce a blaze of colour which will enhance any garden.

OBTAINING PLANTS

The initial plantings will be from plants or tubers which have been given to you or purchased. A reliable method of obtaining this stock is to contact local growers, many of whom will be prepared to sell small quantities of tubers or plants, and a good source of locating these people is to visit dahlia shows where their names will be displayed on prize cards. These growers will be quite prepared to talk to you and to give advice on which varieties to grow.

Failing this there are many nurseries which advertise dahlia tubers for sale. Some are dahlia specialists and others are general nurserymen with a reputation for selling high quality dahlias. It always pays to purchase from the best sources, which do not always charge the highest prices, because the quality will not be evident until the plants are in flower. Unless you are fortunate and live near a supplier it will be necessary to order from a catalogue, so be prepared for some of the varieties to be somewhat different to what you have expected.

COLOURS

A wide range of colours is available, although not necessarily in all forms and sizes. Yellows range from pale cream and lemon through to a rich apricot. Pinks of all shades abound, and there are many different reds from vermilion to a deep crimson. The purple, mauve, violet range is extensive and this runs into lavender and lilac, while oranges, bronzes and autumn toning and various mixtures can be easily obtained. There are a large number of bi-colours in the form of blends and tipped-petal types which are especially popular, and whites are obtainable in most types. With this array it is possible to achieve some dramatic effects, such as a bed of bright scarlet and yellow, a softer arrangement using lavender, rosy pink and white, or an autumn display with orange, bronze and yellow. There is no end to the combinations which are limited only by the imagination of the gardener.

FORM

The shape of the flower which the plants bear is of importance. The forms are described here in fairly simple language.

Pompons are the smallest and neatest of all dahlias, being perfectly spherical like a golf ball with tiny cupped petals. The flowers are usually about 50 mm in diameter, there is a good colour range, and even though the flowers are small they are abundant enough to make a bold showing in the garden.

Cactus dahlias have longish spiky petals which are tubular for part of their length and this gives the flowers a delicate appearance. They come in five sizes ranging from miniature (under 120 mm in diameter) to giant (over 260 mm diameter). These sizes are subject to the amount of disbudding done by growers in order to meet show requirements and will not necessarily achieve these dimensions in the non-specialist's garden, but they are a good indication of what may be expected. There are also varieties called semi-cactus which are similar to cactus but the petals are not as fine and the flower is generally more substantial. These have the same size range as the cactus types.

Fimbriated cactus are similar to the cactus types but have fimbriated or laciniated ends to the petals. In plain words this means that the petals are shaggy, in fact the entire bloom is shaggy and therein lies its charm. The size of these is usually around 160 mm. The colour range is a little restricted but those that are obtainable are well worth their place in the garden, the white varieties being particularly beautiful. There is also a red version which is very striking.

Exhibition cactus are a medium sized cactus type in which the petals are strongly incurved or turned to one side at the tips. There is a limited number of varieties and these are of most interest to the exhibitor as the name suggests. It should not be supposed that they are the only or the best varieties for exhibition - they are not, and it is probably only because exhibitors are always looking for something different that they exist at all. Use them in the garden by all means, but do not look for them to fill your garden.

Decorative types have broader and flatter petals which are set in perfect symmetry and are of a more solid appearance than the cactus types. The sizes are the same as cactus types and the same remarks apply. Decoratives are the most dramatic in appearance of all the dahlias, the ones that attract most attention at shows, and if grown well are the Goliaths of both the show bench and the garden. In the smaller sizes they can be delicate and dainty and the perfection of the petal placement is emphasised. Whether it be to enjoy something that comes as near to perfection as you are liable to get or to impress the neighbours with their immensity the decorative is deserving of a place in any garden.

Waterlily types are so named because they resemble the waterlily, which is also the best way of describing them. They were formerly known as Nymphae which is the botanical name for the waterlily. The size is around 120 mm and most of the colours are delicate, but there are a few which are bold and striking.

Ball type dahlias are similar to the small and miniature decoratives, any differences are of a technical nature and for garden display purposes they may be regarded as decoratives.

Collerettes are a single bloom with an inner circle (or collar) of smaller petals in a contrasting colour. Having fewer petals than the other types they do not have the same depth and are almost flat. The majority are brightly coloured with reds and yellows predominating both as single colours and blends.

Bedding dahlias come in a number of types all of which are dwarf in habit, multi-coloured, and suitable for either bedding or edging. They are not of named varieties and are usually grown from seed.

There are a number of other varieties which are grown, these being anemone, orchid and stellar types. These are unlikely to be grown for garden display but may be included as a novelty.

PRUNING AND DISBUDDING

The shaping of plants in the early stages is important, and the pinching out of the centre of the plant is the first stage of this. This pinching out should be done when the first buds appear at the top of the plant or when the plant reaches 300 mm in height, and it is vital that this is not neglected. The effect of this operation is to cause shoots to branch from the laterals and form a dense bush rather than a straggly plant, and although the first flowers will be delayed the full flush of flowers will be advanced.

Any further pruning or disbudding is done in order to increase the size and quality of the flowers. Each stem of the plant will have a central or main bud with two smaller side buds. Other side buds will also grow at the leaf joints below the main bud cluster. As a general rule of thumb miniature blooms do not need any disbudding, small blooms require one set of the side buds to be removed and for medium or large blooms up to two or three sets of the side buds should be removed. This procedure may seem complicated at first but after a little practise it will become easier, it is basically a matter of removing buds to increase the size of blooms and encourage growth from lower down the plant. The dahlia is a very forgiving plant in this respect and it is most unlikely that a beginner would disbud too heavily, in fact the reverse is more likely to be the case.

During the growing season the main task will be to remove any blooms that are passed their best, or 'dead-heading' as it is called. If seeds pods are allowed to develop the flowering season will be shortened and the size and quality of blooms will decline. The removal of dead flowers, if carried out properly, can also form part of the pruning of plants to encourage new growth.

PESTS AND DISEASES

Dahlias are subject to attacks by pests just like any other plants, and it may be said that because there is always plenty of new succulent growth they are at the top of the menu for the leaf-eating grubs and insects. There are also a number of diseases that may appear. These will not worry the owner of a garden display as much as the exhibitor.

Even the brief details given here may seem complex to the beginner, but this is no more so than the requirements for growing any other plant in the garden. In reality the amount of effort put into growing dahlias is repaid many-fold and there will be rich rewards for the time invested.

Mistakes will be made and some disappointment will be experienced but there will be no regrets. Mistakes can be corrected and disappointments will be more than outweighed by the successes.

5 FEEDING AND WATERING

FEEDING

When we plant dahlias we have high, but not unreasonable, expectations. We will be expecting them to grow to a height of well over a meter in about ten weeks and then produce masses of quite sizeable flowers continuously for a further eight to ten weeks. We will be constantly cutting off blooms to place in vases or on the show bench, and at the same time we will expect the plant to develop a large clump of tubers. It is therefore to be expected that a plant which will use so much energy will have a healthy appetite, or in gardening parlance will be a 'gross feeder'. This is not to say that we should throw large quantities of manures and fertilizers on the plants, regardless of type, and hope for the best. One grower of many years standing advised 'give them plenty of everything and let them take what they want', but this needs to be tempered with a little common sense because, as with many living things, what they like to feed on is not always what is good for them. The following remarks set out to explain what is good for the dahlia, at least the dahlias we want to grow, and how to make sure they get this.

CHEMICAL FERTILIZERS

All fertilizers, whether they be chemical or organic, will contain at least one of the three most basic nutrients - nitrogen (N), phosphorus (P), and potassium (K). Some will contain all three in various quantities, and may also contain other beneficial elements. On manufactured chemical fertilizers there is shown a brief analysis called the NPK analysis, and this gives the percentages of the main elements, e.g. 5-10-5. They may also specify what other elements are present, but the NPK figure is the most important.

Nitrogen is the element which will produce soft green growth and is wonderful for such things as cabbages and lettuce. For dahlias it is very necessary for growth but only to a limited extent. An excess of nitrogen will produce heavy growth and healthy foliage, will tend to delay flowering but increase the size of flowers, and to some extent will improve the colour. It will also cause the stems to be soft and inclined to bend, and too much will cause the tubers to lack keeping qualities. Nitrogen is therefore an element which is essential but which must not be overdone.

There are many sources of nitrogen. All animal manures contain some, particularly when fresh, and blood and bone mixture contains 14% nitrogen in a form which is released slowly. There is a wide range of chemical fertilizers which contain high percentages of nitrogen, some of which are very fast acting, and these should only be used with great caution on dahlias. If a chemical must be used sulphate of ammonia, which contains 22% nitrogen, is perhaps the safest, and could be applied at the rate of 40 grams per square metre. The rate for blood and bone can be three times this amount.

Phosphorus is the element which encourages root growth, strengthens the tissues of the plant, and helps in the formation of fruit and seed. In the dahlia it is vital for the production of strong sturdy plants, the growth of a healthy and extensive root system, and ultimately the tubers on which next year's crop depends. It also tends to advance flowering. Although contained in a number of fertilizers the main source is superphosphate, and it is easy to apply and control in this form. Application rate is 40 to 100 grams per square metre for single superphosphate which contains 20% phosphorus. Triple superphosphate contains up to 48%, and should be used with great care.

Potassium strengthens stems, improves both the colour and size of flowers, supplies the starch which ripens the tubers, and is one of the most important requirements of the dahlia. It will offset the undesirable effects of nitrogen and is useful for stabilising growth if too much nitrogen has been used. There is a slight problem that can arise if an excessive amount is applied, this being the creation of a magnesium deficiency. To overcome this a little magnesium sulphate (Epsom Salts) should be applied. A number of fertilizers contain potassium in small quantities, but it is best introduced in the form of either muriate of potash or sulphate of potash. Of these the sulphate is preferred. The muriate has a higher potash content, but also contains some sodium chloride (salt), and is fairly slow acting, being more suited for application during the winter. The sulphate is quite fast acting, is purer, but is more expensive. The application rate is around 20 to 40 grams per square metre for both types. Wood ash contains potash only in small quantities and needs to be applied at the rate of about 300 to 400 grams per square metre.

In addition to the above there are a number of elements which are essential to growth but which are required only in minute quantities and are known as trace elements. These are usually present naturally, particularly if compost and animal manures are used, but are obtainable from nurseries in the form of a foliar spray. One element is needed in slightly larger quantities and that is iron.

This is provided by sulphate of iron at the rate of 10 grams per square metre.

If chemical fertilizers are to be used it is convenient to make up a mixture which will suit the specific requirements of the dahlia. A recipe for such a mixture is:

> 5 parts blood and bone
> 3 parts superphosphate
> 2 parts sulphate of potash
> (all quantities by weight)
> To each 10 litre bucketful of this mixture add:
> 400 grams of magnesium sulphate
> 100 grams of sulphate of iron

A ready-made mixture with an NPK analysis of 5-10-5 can be purchased. However, this mixture will probably use muriate of potash and may well use sulphate of ammonia as part of the nitrogen component, but is unlikely to have the magnesium and iron components.

The best way of satisfying the fertilizer situation is to buy the individual items in bulk, make up the mixture as it is required, and store the surplus in dry conditions for the next season. This means that the individual items will be on hand when you need to use only one of them, and the cost will be lower.

ORGANIC FERTILIZERS

Organic fertilizers are those which have their origins in plant or animal matter, and these not only provide nutrients but also put humus into the soil to improve the texture, supply some of the trace elements, and introduce a number of useful organisms. Included in this category are animal manures of all types, compost, sea weed, green crops, and blood and bone. Many of the materials which are used as a mulch have not been classified as fertilizers because they give little in the way of nutrients until they have decomposed.

There are other fertilizers which are classed as organic and they are proprietary brands which are produced from animal manures, fish waste, seaweed and the like. They are usually more concentrated in their nutrient content than manures in their natural state and do not provide the same quantities of humus and beneficial organisms. They are very easy to use and are valuable if natural manure is not available, but some types have a high nitrogen content and these should be used with care.

With dahlias, as with most plants, the use of organic material is an essential part of their culture and almost all leading growers make a point of ensuring that their beds get a generous dressing each year. The concentration of beneficial elements in organic fertilizers is far less than in the chemical fertilizers, for example good quality compost would have an NPK analysis of about 1.5 : 0.5 : 1.0. The application rate for this would need to be 3 kg per square metre and will require the addition of superphosphate (P) to provide balance. Animal manures have NPK figures that are closer to compost than to a 5:10:5 mixture, but this low quantity of nutrients should not deter the grower from using organic material as much as possible. Soil is a living substance and in nature is continually receiving organic material from decaying plant and animal life to maintain the micro-organisms that keep it fertile. This is something that no amount of chemical fertilizing can achieve, particularly if it is to be cropped as heavily and intensively as the dahlia beds.

LIQUID FERTILIZERS

No discussion on fertilizers would be complete without some mention of the wide range of liquid fertilizers that are available. It seems that almost every agricultural chemical company in existence has developed the ideal solution to all problems of nutrition of all plants. That these products are most effective, easy to use, quick acting, and moderately low in cost (if purchased in bulk) is not doubted. What should be of some concern to the dahlia grower is whether they will provide the right type of nutrition at the appropriate time of the season. We do not want a flush of soft foliar growth when we are trying to produce strong stems just prior to the shows. Some of the products are available in different grades and contain differing ratios of the essential elements, but others are just general growth boosters, so look at the NPK analysis before you buy.

The old fashioned liquid fertilizer made by steeping a sack of animal manure in water for a week or so is still of great value, especially if a good handful of potash is put into the sack. This needs to be diluted before use. It should be the colour of weak tea when it is used.

A FEEDING PROGRAM

A very suitable fertilizing plan is to combine organic and chemical fertilizers, using the organic substances to produce soil which is both fertile and of good texture and the chemicals to provide the required elements at the appropriate time. There are many variations of how this should be put into practice, but the following is a schedule that has proven most satisfactory in the past.

After lifting tubers in the winter remove all dahlia stems to prevent the spread of disease and dig the beds, turning in any annual weeds and the remnants of any mulch that has been applied. If a green crop is to be grown this can now be sown and the beds dressed with any organic material available. At this stage it is unlikely that any amount would be too much but a dressing of about 75 to 100 mm deep would be about the right quantity. This can be topped off with a dressing of lime (dolomite limestone for preference) at the rate of 200 grams per square meter and the bed left in a rough dug state until about six weeks before the planned planting date. In that time the organic fertilizer will have matured and rotted to some extent, earth worms will have started to carry out their valuable work, and the green crop (if planted) should be ready to dig in. The second digging should be done with a fork and the texture be left a little finer than the winter digging. Some two weeks before the planting date the final digging can be done, but if the ground is wet it is advisable to delay this until conditions are drier. If a chemical fertilizer is to be used it can be either broadcast on the bed at this stage or placed where the plants or tubers will be planted as soon as the stakes are in position. The application rate for the mixture described previously should be 80 to 100 grams per square metre or to each planting position.

After about ten weeks of growth a further application of mixture can be applied at the same rate, but be sure that the ground is moist before applying any fertilizer to growing plants and water well afterwards. This should be sufficient to ensure good strong growth all through the season, but it may be necessary to give additional potash in mid-summer if the stems are weak, and this is best given as a tight handful (80 grams) to 10 litres of water and watered into the ground using 1½ to 2 litres per plant. It is also beneficial to give a dressing of superphosphate at the rate of 100 grams per square meter towards the end of the flowering period to assist in producing healthy tubers.

The application of mulch to conserve moisture should not form a part of the feeding program. Stable manures used in mulching should not be fresh when applied, because if fresh they will introduce nitrogen at a time when the need for nitrogen has passed. If mulch with any significant nutrient content is used the feeding program must take account of this.

The above program could be augmented or partially replaced by the use of liquid fertilizers, of the correct type, as a foliar feed. This is a particularly useful idea during the early life of a plant when the roots are still small and unable to take up very much nutrient and later in the season if the growth is not as it should be. One of the virtues of this foliar feeding is that the results will be seen in two or three days instead of the two or three weeks it takes for conventional fertilizing to show a result. If using this method it is important that the rates specified by the maker are not exceeded. Over feeding can cause very real problems, and the maker is not likely to advise that his product be underused. These comments about over feeding apply to all methods. It is always best to feed little and often, and because it is so important to avoid over feeding (which is done far too frequently) the subject is dealt with in some detail here.

Plants take up nutrients through minute and delicate root hairs from nutrient salts which are contained in water. There is no other way that roots can take up food through the root system. The way in which this occurs is through a complex system called osmosis. The membrane of the root hairs will allow water to pass through them, thus the nutrients in the water pass into the plant to be used in building stems and leaves and flower buds. The root hairs have a means of concentrating the nutrient salts so that there is always a good supply in the root of the plant. The important thing about osmosis is that the flow will always be from a weak solution to a strong solution. In the case of a well-balanced condition this will be from the weak solution (moisture) surrounding the roots to the strong solution within the root. This enables the root to pass the nutrient-laden sap up the plant and to use the nutrient-laden water to replenish its stock of concentrated nutrient. This will only happen when the nutrient balance is in this state. If the balance is disturbed osmosis will not just cease it will be reversed. If a strong nutrient solution is fed to the roots the flow of water will be from the weaker sap in the root hairs to the higher nutrient-laden water in the soil. The effect of this is that the plant gets no food, the root hairs are drained of moisture and collapse and very soon there is no plant to worry about.

This is a very much simplified explanation of a complicated subject, but the message is quite simple and clear - do not over feed. Any over feeding that occurs is likely to be the result of using liquid fertilizers at the root. Organic and chemical fertilizers take a longer time to become available in a liquid form and are not likely to flood the roots with nutrient-laden moisture. Using a liquid fertilizer at a greater strength than is recommended is at the root of most of the evils, as is feeding plants that are looking sickly.

If a plant has been overfed and is showing symptoms of distress on no account should it be given more food. The only thing that can be done is to water copiously to wash away some of the nutrients in the soil, and perhaps apply a foliar feed.

All growers with a few years of experience have sorted out their feeding problems and have developed a program that suits their particular situation. They have come to know their soil well and through trial and error have arrived at a method which gives the results that they are seeking. However, it is of no use for the beginner to blindly follow their way of doing things because there may be a major difference in soil types which will make a program that is suitable in one area totally unsuitable in another.

The most advisable course for the beginner to take is to use ample organic material, use the chemical fertilizers in moderation, be very wary of using liquid fertilizers for application at the roots, take note of the results and make any adjustments in small steps. In this way it will not be long before an effective and safe feeding program has been established.

To add further confusion to the whole question of feeding dahlia plants it must be stated that there are some varieties, mainly in the miniature range, that do not produce good results if they are well fed. This is particularly evident when attempting to grow for show purposes when it is found that varieties which are miniatures grow oversized. This is another area where experience, or advice from experienced growers, will provide an answer.

The whole question of feeding plants can be as simple or as complicated as the gardener cares to make it. For some it will be a question of finding a suitable method and sticking to it. Others may wish to pursue the matter further, and for those who follow this path there is ample literature for them to study. Much of this literature is produced by government departments responsible for research and providing advice on agricultural matters, and their publications are usually clear, concise, understandable and obtainable at a reasonable cost.

The beginner should understand that the main objective of feeding is to promote strong and steady growth to produce a healthy and robust plant, for it is only from such plants that the best of blooms will come. Size alone is no indication of health, and within a short time the methods of manipulating fertilizing methods in order to produce the ideal plants will become evident.

WATERING

The dahlia is a plant that requires plenty of water during its growing period but does not like to have water standing around the roots or having stale water in the ground. Watering, therefore, is closely associated with drainage, and it is often thought of by many as being a matter of making sure that beds are well drained and then applying water in copious quantities. This is an over simplification of the situation because although there is nothing very scientific about watering a garden there are one or two points which must be noted.

When tubers are planted the soil should be moist but not wet. The tuber will contain enough moisture to serve the needs of the shoot and the small plant until it is about 75 mm to 100mm high. It is not until this time that there will be any roots to take up the moisture, so it will certainly not do any good. On the other hand, to place a tuber in wet conditions is a sure way to make it rot, and tuber rot is perhaps the greatest threat to the young plants at this stage of growth. It therefore follows that tubers and plants grown from tubers should not be watered until those plants are 100 mm high. The only exception is if the weather is extremely hot and dry, the soil is dry to a depth of 150 mm, and there is danger of the tuber withering because of these conditions.

When plants grown from cuttings are planted they will have roots, very tender roots, and these should be watered when planted and never allowed to dry out.

Where a mixture of green plants and tubers are planted individual treatment must be given. It is not possible to use a sprinkler system until all plants are at the stage where they require watering.

After the plants have grown to about 150 mm high they should be watered generously and not allowed to dry out. From this stage until the flower buds start to develop it is beneficial to allow water to spray on to the foliage, especially after a hot day. Watering is best carried out in early morning before the sun gets too hot or in the evenings, the mornings being preferred so that the plants will not remain wet during the cool of the night. After flowers start to open the water should be sprayed over the foliage but not on the flowers. Water will not cause the leaves to burn through sun shining on them while they are wet, but it will cause some staining or even burning of the petals, making them unfit for showing.

The amount of water and frequency of watering will depend on the type of soil, light or sandy soil needing more frequent applications than heavier soils. There are meters and other devices to test moisture levels, but it is not really difficult to tell whether soil is moist or not. One thing that should be watched carefully is that water is actually getting into the ground and not just running off, a situation that can occur when a mulch becomes compacted and resistant to water.

A sign of insufficient water is the wilting of plants, and although this is cured with a good soaking it is not good to allow the plant to dry out to this extent because this will cause uneven growth and the plant will never be as good as one which has been grown without any interruption. All plants will wilt a little after a very hot day, but if supplied with sufficient water will soon revive in the cool of the evening, and a spray of water over the plant will assist this revival.

It should be noted that wilting is also an indication of over watering, and if the ground has become too wet it must be allowed to dry out until the plant recovers. Whether wilting is caused by too little or too much moisture will be indicated by the state of the soil, but if there is no moisture problem the cause of the wilting may be more serious and the reason for it must be sought.

As with all plants a good soaking that gets right down to the feeding roots, once or twice a week, is much better than a sprinkling every day. With the latter there is always a danger that the soil at root level will be dry and the roots will turn upwards in an attempt to reach the surface moisture, thus exposing them to the surface heat and any strong fertilizer that may be on the surface of the soil.

If towards the end of the season it is planned to save some seed pods to raise plants from seed the pods should be kept as dry as possible. When flowering is completed the soil should still be kept moist because during this time the tubers are completing their growth.

Watering is often used as a method of making blooms increase in size and on the day before a show it is not uncommon for growers to water lavishly to increase the size of blooms which are too small.

When water has been applied the plants will be particularly brittle and susceptible to damage for the following 12 hours, and this should be borne in mind when working among plants that have been recently watered.

6 PROPAGATION

One of the main concerns of dahlia growers is how to obtain new stock. Beginners will need to satisfy initial requirements and the experienced growers will be seeking new varieties to improve the chances of winning major awards. New stock will probably be available as tubers or as green plants, depending on local practices, and the grower will have to take whatever is available.

When it comes to increasing stock from existing plants it is a very different matter, for the choice is that of the grower, and this is where the newcomer will learn what a versatile and bountiful plant the dahlia can be when it comes to reproducing itself.

There are three means of obtaining new plants - by planting seeds, by planting tubers and by raising them from cuttings. It may well be, that for various reasons, a grower will choose to use all of these methods.

GROWING FROM SEEDS

The dahlias that we grow today are hybrids rather than species and have a very mixed ancestry. Because of this they will not produce progeny from seed that is true to the type of its parents, indeed the results usually obtained from seed often bear little resemblance to the parent plants and are almost always inferior in every respect. To obtain good varieties from seed requires an enormous amount of luck or a great deal of skill and research.

An exception to this is the dwarf bedding dahlias which are often used as edging plants. These are single flowered types in a mixture of colours, and should not be confused with the collerette type. Although plants are usually available from nurseries they are easy to raise from seed sown in a good seed-raising mixture in the spring and treated as annuals. They are frost-sensitive, so they should be given protection and only planted out when any danger of frost is over.

In general the beginner will be bitterly disappointed if an attempt is made to stock the dahlia beds with plants raised from seed, and the growing of seedling plants for this purpose is not recommended. However, almost every dahlia variety in existence originated from seed, this being the usual way of creating new varieties. The raising of seedlings is a fascinating part of dahlia growing which can bring great rewards.

GROWING FROM TUBERS

In regions where the climate is suitable, being neither too hot nor too cold, many growers choose to plant individual tubers as the means of obtaining their plants. Tubers will produce plants which are true to the parent plant and this is probably the easiest method for the beginner to use. Provided that proper planting methods are followed a high success rate will be achieved with the least amount of effort. There have been thousands of champion blooms produced by plants grown from tubers and, although in some circles this method is regarded as inferior, there are many successful exhibitors who rely entirely on tuber plantings.

GROWING FROM CUTTINGS

When tubers are held in store until shoots are produced those shoots may be severed from the tuber and struck as cuttings. These are commonly known as 'green plants', and many growers use this method of propagation for all their stock. These will grow true to the form, colour and size of the parent plant and will, in fact, be exactly the same variety.

The advocates of this method claim that the resulting plants are hardier, more disease resistant and produce better results in general than those grown from tubers. This is supported by the fact that when a variety that has been grown from tubers over a long period appears to be losing vigour or is declining in quality the growing of plants from cuttings will often rejuvenate it.

Where winters are long or springs are too cold to plant out tubers in time to get a reasonably long blooming period before the earliest frosts arrive it is possible to get tubers to shoot and cuttings to root by the use of some protection and warmth. By this means the cuttings will be planted out in milder weather conditions, at a later time than tubers are planted, but as well-rooted plants of about 100 mm high.

There are very good reasons, therefore, to use the cutting or green plant method as the means of raising at least some stock, particularly in areas where the climate does not favour the use of tuber plantings.

A different type of cutting is used in certain circumstances, these being known as late cuttings. This method involves taking cuttings from an established plant during the growing period, and is a useful method of preserving a 'sport', which is an abnormal condition where a part of the plant changes its form or colour. This method may also be used to increase the stock of rare varieties.

METHOD OF PRODUCING GREEN PLANTS

If cuttings are to be taken the tubers, whether they are in clumps or have been divided into individual tubers, are taken from store in early spring and examined for soundness. Any signs of rotting may be cut away and the cut treated with sulphur, but if the rotting is extensive the tuber will have to be discarded.

The tubers should be placed in trays of sandy loam with the tubers covered but the crowns or eyes left uncovered. The loam should be moist without being wet and must be kept in this condition. The trays should then be placed in a glasshouse with bottom heat, or in some other warm position, with ample light and air. The object of this is to convince the tubers that summer has arrived and growth should be started. The eyes and buds will start to appear in a couple of weeks, and in a further two or three weeks they will have developed into shoots about 75 to 100 mm long which will be the cuttings. Needless to say, the tubers should still be well labelled to preserve the identity of the variety.

When the shoots are of the correct length the rooting medium can be prepared, and this should be a 50-50 mixture (by bulk) of peat moss and coarse sand. The peat moss should be wetted before mixing and care should be taken that the sand is free from salt or other harmful impurities. This mixture should be kept moist at all times. Cuttings may be struck in small beds or in pots which have some source of bottom heat and can be covered to create a warm and humid atmosphere. If pots are used glass or plastic jars placed over the pots work very well, and if an electric propagator is available this would be ideal for a small numbers of cuttings.

The cuttings should be severed from the tuber with a razor blade making the cut just below a leaf node (i.e. the junction of a pair of leaves). It is important that this cut is made just below the node and not between nodes, and that the cut be as clean as possible. The bottom pair of leaves should be removed cleanly, and if any of the other leaves are over-large they can also be trimmed. If a hormone rooting powder is to be used the base of the cutting should be dipped into this. It is probable that the cuttings will strike without this treatment, but if it improves the speed or rate of results it is well worth the little effort involved. The reason for cutting the shoot just below a leaf node is that if the cut is made between the nodes it is quite likely that any plant that results will produce tubers that are 'blind', i.e. the tubers will have a normal appearance but will not produce eyes for future propagation. Quite often the second node is chosen as this will allow further shoots to emerge from the first node, thus providing a further supply of cuttings.

7 LIFTING, DIVIDING AND STORING TUBERS

The treatment of tubers at the end of the season is of major importance for it will determine the number and quality of tubers you will have for the following year. As with many other aspects of dahlia growing there are a number of opinions on how and when this should be done, and these are usually influenced by location, climate, experience and personal preference.

It must be said at the outset that dahlia tubers are delicate enough to require gentle handling and are sensitive to storage conditions. All dahlia growers will admit to losses of tubers in the time between lifting and re-planting, but despite this vast quantities survive. For the beginner a large proportion of losses are due to a cavalier attitude in the treatment of tubers. With the requisite knowledge and a moderate amount of care it is quite possible for every grower to successfully lift and store a more than ample supply of tubers.

NEED TO LIFT TUBERS

The first question which arises is whether there is any real need to lift the tubers and it is generally accepted among serious growers that it is in fact necessary. That so many major growers, whose plantings are in the hundreds, consider it essential to undertake the considerable amount of work involved is an indication that there are overwhelming advantages in doing so. It is suggested that in this area the general gardener would be well advised to follow the example of the expert. The reasons why the lifting of tubers each year is considered to be of such importance are:

* Tubers left in the ground will be in danger of rotting in the cold, wet soil during the winter months. They may be affected by heavy frosts and are subject to attack by pests such as slugs, snails and slaters.

* Only by clearing the ground is it possible to prepare the beds for next year's planting. The winter digging and application of organic material and lime, which are so vital to the production of good quality dahlias, can only be carried out if the beds have been cleared. Clearing of beds will, of course, be necessary if a green crop is to be planted.

* If tubers are allowed to remain in the ground during the winter, and survive this treatment, the growth the following year will consist of a number of stems which will not have the strength and vigour of a single stem. The resulting plants will be difficult to manage, blooms will be of poor quality, and the future clumps of tubers will be convoluted and difficult to divide. This is caused by a number of stems attempting to draw nourishment from a small and under prepared area of ground. In addition there will also be a risk of the plant growing from tubers which are in the process of rotting, a problem which has been discussed elsewhere.

Even where dahlias are grown only for garden display or for cut flowers the lifting of tubers each year is recommended. In certain circumstances it may be acceptable to leave tubers in the ground for one year, if the danger of loss and reduction in quality can be tolerated, but to leave them longer than this is most inadvisable.

TIME OF LIFTING

It is frequently stated that tubers should be lifted when the plants have been blackened by frost, and while this is quite true it should not be considered as the only indication that lifting time has arrived. There are districts which are not subject to heavy frosts, in some years the frosts may be late, and some plants may be grown in positions which are sheltered. In such cases it would be futile to await some event which may not occur and it is much more reasonable to establish a logical timing for lifting. The time to lift tubers is when they have matured and ripened sufficiently but before the ground has become wet and cold to the extent that damage is likely to occur. There is a risk in lifting tubers that have not matured sufficiently because they are liable to shrink and wither in storage and fail to shoot the following year. About six weeks after the last of the flowers have gone and the foliage has turned brown or has yellowed to a significant degree is about the right time to lift. If mid-winter arrives and the foliage is still green then it may be necessary to help things along a little. This can be done by inserting a garden fork in the soil adjacent (but not too adjacent) to the clump and lifting it sufficiently to break the feeding roots. The effect of this is to stop any further flow of sap to the foliage and after a couple of weeks the clump should be ready to lift.

LIFTING PROCEDURES

One of the things to bear in mind during lifting is that it is important to keep varieties separated and properly labelled. The best way of achieving this is to set about the task in an orderly manner so that you do not end up with foliage, stakes and tubers lying all over the garden.

First remove all ties from the plants, cut off the foliage to within 200 mm of the ground and remove the bulk of weed growth from the beds. Then transfer the labels from the stakes to the shortened stems, or fix separate labels on them, making sure that they are firmly fixed and the writing will not fade or become washed off. Then, and only then, the stakes should be removed. If the stakes are firmly in the ground it will be found that by driving them in a little bit more they will be easier to remove.

When the stakes have been taken away it is time to start the actual lifting, and this is where care is needed. The tubers are very brittle and will snap off the clump or be damaged at the slightest suggestion of rough handling, so do not attempt to hurry the job or lift too many at one time. Many varieties produce tubers with long slender necks and these are particularly liable to breakage. Needless to say, tubers with broken necks are useless.

The first step for each clump is to take a sharp spade and push it full depth into the soil all around the clump, which will extend about 200 mm from the stem in all directions, thus making a circular cut some 400 mm across. While doing this make a slight lifting motion with the spade with each cut to help to release the clump from the ground. When the clump has been loosened it should be lifted clear of the hole and it is often a help to use two spades to do this. The clump should on no account be lifted by the stump at this stage, the weight of the tubers and soil will be too much for the stem to bear. The amount of soil adhering to the tubers will vary according to the texture and condition of the ground and some of it will need to be removed. If there is a large amount of soil the bulk of it should be removed at this stage by probing with a blunt stick, taking care not to damage tubers or to disturb the clump too much.

The next step depends on whether the clump is to be divided into single tubers for storing immediately or stored whole and divided later. In any case try to leave the clump without moving it around for two or three hours. Even in this short time the tubers will start to harden and be less liable to damage.

DIVIDING TUBER CLUMPS

There are two main methods of dealing with tubers from this point on, either dividing the tubers immediately and storing them away or storing the tubers as a clump to be divided at some later time when the shoots start to appear. Both of these methods have advantages and disadvantages, and the success in terms of tubers surviving the storage period is just about equal for both methods. The choice will depend on which method suits the preference of the grower and, of course, there is no reason why both methods should not be used.

The advantages in dividing into individual tubers at the time of digging are that the tubers are soft and fairly easy to cut, a large number of divided tubers can be stored in a small space, and it saves valuable time in the spring when there are many jobs to be done in the garden.

The advantage of storing the clumps whole is that the only tubers which are cut, named, treated, and stored are those which have survived the winter, are showing signs of growth, and have every chance of developing into satisfactory plants.

If it is intended that plants will be raised from cuttings rather than from planted tubers the storing of tuber clumps would be the most satisfactory method.

To divide the tubers it will first be necessary to wash them with a soft jet from a hose to remove all soil in order to see the shoots or eyes. At this stage there is need for a little knowledge of how new growth in the dahlia is generated. The dahlia is not a true tuber, like the potato, as it does not have eyes or buds on the swollen root from which new growth will emerge. The new growth will come from the swollen base of the stem, called the crown, just above the tubers. This growth is initially in the form of an embryo bud, called an eye, which develops into a bud and eventually a shoot. Sometimes the eyes are fairly high up on the crown and in other instances they appear quite low down towards the neck of the tubers. To be of any use a tuber must have attached to it an eye and a piece of the crown sufficient to support it. Some practice is required in identifying the eyes. When the tubers are first lifted it is comparatively easy to distinguish them, but after a day or so they will recede, only to appear again in the spring. When clumps are stored until the spring the eyes will develop into buds or shoots and are quite visible. They are also very fragile and extra care will be needed when dividing and handling.

Cutting is done with a strong, sharp knife, and secateurs are also useful. There are also times when a particularly large clump may call for a small saw to reduce it to manageable proportions before division can be made. By looking carefully at the clump it will be possible to see tubers which have an eye attached and these may be removed, making sure that each tuber has a piece of stem with an eye attached to it. As tubers are removed others will be revealed, and these also can be removed, until all suitable tubers have been separated from the clump. Care should be taken in handling the tubers, which are still delicate, and it is better to make sure of cutting one very good tuber instead of two doubtful ones.

Having divided the clumps into individual tubers they should now be prepared for storage. Any small wispy roots are cut off and the tubers are generally tidied up. At this stage many growers dip the tubers into a solution of fungicide, allowing them to soak for about five minutes. All cut surfaces should be coated with sulphur powder to help them to dry out and prevent rot from starting. When doing this it is advisable to avoid letting the sulphur come into contact with eyes or shoots as there is some evidence to suggest that sulphur is likely to damage the eyes.

Each tuber needs to be identified by writing the name of the variety on it. This has traditionally been done with an indelible pencil but a felt-tipped marker pen is satisfactory provided it is a waterproof type. The tubers are now ready for storing, but before this is done they should be allowed to dry out for a few days. If they are stored in a wet condition there will be a tendency for rotting to occur.

From the above it will be realized that a considerable amount of handling of tubers is involved. Care should be taken while doing this and touching of the eyes or shoots should be avoided. It is also important to avoid mixing tubers during these operations and a good way of doing this is to handle only one variety at a time or obtain a separate tray or container for each variety and keep the name label with the tubers at all times.

STORAGE OF DIVIDED TUBERS

Tubers divided immediately after lifting will need to be stored for some months whereas those that are divided at a later time will not be so long in store. Boxes that will not disintegrate if damp will be required to hold the tubers. Those made from cardboard will not be suitable, wooden boxes will suffice unless they are too heavy, but the ideal boxes are those made from polystyrene foam in which fruit is transported.

There are a number of materials which are suitable for use as a storage medium, the common element among these being that they have some capacity to retain moisture. These include sand, sawdust, sphagnum moss and peat moss. If sand is used it should be the sharp kind which will not pack hard. The softer mediums are more satisfactory when the time comes for removing tubers from storage. The crucial factor is the moisture level of the medium which should be damp. If too wet there is danger of tubers rotting, if too dry the tubers may wither and shrink.

Tubers should be packed neatly into the boxes, making sure that they are all in contact with the storage medium. It will be a help if all boxes are labelled with the varieties they contain, and if they are stacked to make sure they are not stacked too high. Storage in a shed or under cover is recommended.

Even though the initial moisture level may be correct it will not stay this way over the storage period. It is necessary to examine the boxes every few weeks to check the moisture level and dampen the medium if it is too dry. It is also advisable to look at the tubers from time to time and remove any that are showing signs of rotting.

STORAGE OF TUBER CLUMPS

Where the climate is mild tuber clumps are often allowed to spend the winter outdoors. In this situation there is still some need to ensure that the clumps do not dry out and this is usually achieved with a covering of soil. This covering should not be too deep or the same conditions as leaving tubers in the ground would apply. These clumps will require some protection from pests, slugs and snails being the main offenders. It has also been known for larger animals to make inroads into the crop.

If tuber clumps are to be stored outdoors where there is a danger of frosts or heavy rain it will be necessary to provide some extra protection, perhaps in the form of plastic sheeting. In such cases particular care should be taken with labels, which must be durable enough to withstand the elements. It is usual to reduce the stem to about 50 mm and place the clump upside-down for a few days to allow excess moisture to drain out. The clump should then be pierced down through the stem with a screwdriver to ensure complete drainage and stored with the stem uppermost with only the actual tubers covered with soil.

When clumps which have been stored are to be divided the same procedures should be followed as when dividing clumps at lifting time. Extra care will be needed to avoid damage to any shoots or buds that have emerged. Even though the tubers may be planted almost immediately it is still necessary to apply sulphur to all cut surfaces and the naming of individual tubers is recommended to avoid any confusion.

COMMON PROBLEMS

During the process of dividing and storing tubers it is possible that some difficulties will arise that the beginner is unable to cope with. There are a few common problems which are frequently encountered which can be dealt with by simple methods.

When a lifted tuber clump is very large and convoluted it may be impossible to determine how best to divide it. In such a situation the normal procedure of detaching tubers one by one is not suitable, and it will be necessary to cut the entire clump in half or into four. It should then be easier to see where a start can be made.

A plant that has been lifted may have no tubers of any substance, being composed of very thin tubers or wispy roots. Any tubers or roots cut from this will have little chance of survival, and if the variety is common and plentiful it is hardly worth bothering with. If, however, it is a rare or special variety the entire root system should immediately be planted in a pot with moist soil, the pot being given the usual care given to tubers and kept moist but not wet. With some luck shoots will be produced in the spring and these can be used for cuttings to provide further plants.

During an examination of the tubers in storage signs of rotting may be detected. All tubers in that box should be removed and examined, rotten tubers discarded, those just starting to rot may be cut back to sound tuber and treated with sulphur. The tubers should be allowed to dry out for a few days if they are too wet and repacked in fresh medium.

Unfortunately there will always be tubers which will rot despite all due care being taken. There are some varieties which are notoriously hard to keep and in some years seem to produce more problems in this regard than others. This latter appears to be due to climatic conditions during the growing period, but another cause of tubers rotting is the use of fertilizers with a high nitrogen content.

GARDEN HYGIENE

There is always a possibility of diseases being carried over from one year to another via the foliage which is removed from plants if this is dug into the ground or used in the compost heap. Many growers remove or burn every trace of foliage, others will use foliage in the compost only if it is healthy, and still others will compost foliage but refrain from using the composted material on dahlia beds.

There are some diseases which render the plant material totally unsuitable for anything but removal or burning, notably Stem Rot (Sclerotina) and Virus Wilt Disease, although these plants should have been removed when the disease was first noticed.

After lifting tubers the beds should be dug over, and at this time make sure that any tubers that may have been broken off during lifting are removed.

Although the process of preparing tubers for the following season may seem a little complex it is well worth the effort. Nothing can be worse than starting off a new season having to acquire new stock because most of the tubers have been lost due to lack of care in dividing and storing. Growers with little experience in this area will find it beneficial to contact an experienced grower for advice and guidance, for no amount of written instruction will replace a practical demonstration by an expert.

John Allport died in May 2013.

Although he gained much satisfaction from growing and exhibiting dahlias, John's main focus was on assisting and mentoring other growers. He was always generous with his advice and it was his intention to produce a written guide to pass on his knowledge. Ill-health prevented him from seeing it through to completion.

This book has been published in John's memory by the Dahlia Section of the Hobart Horticultural Society.

CPSIA information can be obtained
at www.ICGtesting.com
Printed in the USA
BVHW020225161020
591185BV00001B/1